VISCERA

Felice Belle is a writer of brevity and power. Her poems explore—among many things—pandemic isolation, heartbreak and loss, cultural collisions, dreams, desire and artistry. *Viscera* is Felice Belle talking to us, and it is urgent and beautiful.

—Jessica Hagedorn

Whimsically masterful, moving, and profound, *Viscera* is a collection that captivates you with every poem. Belle delves into the raw heart of magic and memory, pop culture and physics. This is an unforgettable journey, distinguished by exquisitely crafted poems on love and loss that time-travel between train rides and trips to the moon. Belle is a voice to be celebrated, who with every page turn breaks and then restores your ragged heart.

—Jennifer Murphy, *First Responder*

Viscera by Felice Belle does what time machines are meant to do—remind us of who we are while encouraging and affirming who we've become. Felice's voice is so clear and so distinct that I was transported instantly back in time, sitting in an audience at her feet. Her poetry is deceptive. It comforts you with soft clever rhymes, while stealthily delivering emotional and weighted gut punches. I found myself near tears more often than I'm sure she intended. I read the entire book with my hand clutching my chest. I laughed and I cried and I remembered people I've loved and lost and lost and loved—but that hand never left my chest just as this book will never leave my heart. I've been waiting 20 years for Felice Belle to give the world a book of her poems. I cannot wait for the world to welcome her into their lives. *Viscera* will leave you longing for times when your friends were the loves of your life and every joy and heartbreak was just another reason to write a poem. This book is a comfort.

—Bassey Ikpi, *New York Times* Bestseller,
I'm Telling the Truth but I'm Lying

Felice Belle's poetry dances across the pages, animated by the joys and challenges of personal and political life, of romance, family, and friendship. The everyday and the ecstatic are both vividly rendered here, and the poems are vibrant odes to New York and to black music. *Viscera* is a collection built from an intoxicating range of references, beautifully constellated, delivered with intelligent soundplay and a powerfully beating heart.

—Jamel Brinkley, *Witness*

Felice Belle is a visionary poet who refuses to let loss and the daily absurdities of New York City microaggressions get her down. Belle's poems are wickedly funny, full of sharp dialogue and precise imagery. There is a casual conversational elegance in *Viscera* that brings me so deeply close to a poet who is on top of her craft spilling truths from the mug of shattering heartbreak. Belle does what is very hard to do during the downside-up time: she takes a deep soulful breath when the daily WTF moments get in the way and channels herself to say, "your canon is not my canon / your war is not my war / your voice is not my voice," yet with all the differences between us there is a heartbeat of hope that inspires and ignites us to be gracious to one another during these unprecedented times.

—Regie Cabico, Nuyorican Poets Café
Grand Slam Champion and Theater Artist

Early in *Viscera*, Felice Belle tells us "your suffering is unique / and you are not alone in it"—which serves as a compelling invitation into the boldness, power, and emotional reach of this collection. Here are poems of searching—for recognition, belonging, affirmation, power, and love—and of finding each through great effort and patience, and ultimately through self-acceptance and self-discovery. Belle says, "but i am an against-the-odds kind of girl" and then admits "i don't want the preacher / i want the pulpit." Indeed, these poems—riding the ambitious spirits of Prince, Drake, and Whitman—speak into the soul and inspire us all to stand taller, and braver too, especially in times of distress and heartache. It's no wonder that as the book comes to a close, Belle triumphantly reminds herself (and us) that "you were born for such a time as this."

—Faisal Mohyuddin,
The Displaced Children of Displaced Children

VISCERA

Felice Belle

Etruscan Press

Etruscan Press
Wilkes University
84 West South Street
Wilkes-Barre, PA 18766
(570) 408-4546

www.etruscanpress.org

Published 2023 by Etruscan Press
Printed in the United States of America
Cover design by Logan Rock
Interior design and typesetting by Aaron Petrovich
The text of this book is set in Sabon Lt Pro

First Edition

17 18 19 20 5 4 3 2 1

Library of Congress Cataloguing-in-Publication Data

Names: Belle, Felice, author.
Title: Viscera / Felice Belle.
Description: First edition. | Wilkes-Barre, PA : Etruscan Press, 2023. | Summary: "Set in New York City, circa now, Viscera chronicles the pursuit of love and unassailable truth in a world designed to deny one's humanity. Our poet protagonist interrogates the cultural belief systems that bind and ultimately finds freedom in relentless self-definition. Inspired by pop culture patron saints and crime procedurals, Viscera investigates how to transfigure a fractured soul into a fully realized mosaic. From intimate whisper to wry conversation to Whitmanesque prophecy, Felice Belle's voice speaks to, and for, and somehow from us-as we are now-'never...more separate' and 'never...more connected.' These poems inhabit a frontier beyond free verse, yet thrum with an orality older than the alphabet. Viscera pays homage to the heart and cuts to the bone. It celebrates the multitudes within and the exquisite inherent risk in composing a life"-- Provided by publisher.
Identifiers: LCCN 2022028388 | ISBN 9798985882407 (paperback ; acid-free paper)
Subjects: LCGFT: Poetry.
Classification: LCC PS3602.E45738 V57 2022 | DDC 811/.6--dc23/eng/20220616
LC record available at https://lccn.loc.gov/2022028388

Please turn to the back of this book for a list of the sustaining funders of Etruscan Press.

This book is printed on recycled, acid-free paper.

"Healing is an act of communion."
–bell hooks

for the love

Table of Contents

Acknowledgements

The author gratefully acknowledges the following publications where these poems first appeared:

African Voices — "rockaway" (as "for peter in far rockaway")

Brooklyn Poets — "you are here."

Bum Rush the Page: A Def Poetry Jam — "exceptions"

The Common — "postcard from the moon" and "the distance between you and me"

Long Shot — "next lifetime"

Overpass — "yours as much as mine"

Sad Vacation — "gambling"

Slam — "baby, it's cold outside"

VISCERA

postcard from the moon

everything is normal

in space
your heart shrinks

like an astronaut
writing folks back home
a skeleton in a wig
with nowhere to go

washing dishes in a volcano
humming the ever-present
elevator music of anxiety

what does the science say?

we are living history
i only want to hear from people with degrees in it
there has never been enough time
i call everyone who has ever been on my mind

the story can save or destroy
how do you want to play this?

we're not ready for a black *jeopardy* host
it is a sign of progress

your suffering is unique
and you are not alone in it

we know the thing
before it is named

if you spot the con
is it even a game?

the systems we serve break
because they weren't designed
for us to survive

nothing is normal

the head and the heart were never not one

the woman who wants to travel
will find transportation

sunday afternoon in harlem

the cab driver asks
what my favorite position
is. no tip given.

next lifetime

my mind is being fucked consistently
the rest of my body is getting jealous
like your father

who refused to eat tomatoes
from the tree your mother's lover
planted in your backyard

we ate that fruit religiously
received each piece
like communion bread

do this for the remembrance of me

today there will be no
hand wavin'
no foot stompin'
no spirits being gotten

for the remembrance of me
i reincarnate myself

uptown harlem brown
black man with wisdom-colored curls
and creased face say,
hey, soldier, what's going on?

he saw war in my eyes
wanted to know
what i was fighting for

just your everyday defensive
i say bye, mouth twisted wry
flash peace sign
decide i'm reincarnating myself

today, shed dead socialized skin
hand-me-down habits
passed through generations
mothering men whose cords ain't been cut yet
persecuted when flashing inappropriate amounts
of leg and/or intellect

too grown to play dumb
play dead for no one
instead, play big boy games
for a taste of that male privilege
i hear so much about

still the odd woman out

put on my poker face
the dealer called spades
said rules were meant to change
with the game and i've forgotten
what i'm playing for

so i create imaginary playmates
who challenge me
to mold this reality
like fluorescent colored play-doh

i put faith in myself
so when i'm let down
i know who to blame

i talk to myself
when no one wants to hear
what i have to say

i talk to myself out loud
so you're going to have to listen anyway

today, didn't have the energy to reincarnate
i needed a hug, a foot rub, your love
(in that order)

perfection is a perception
exists only in your head
and all the saints i know are dead
that is a prerequisite for sainthood

good samaritans get greedy
sometimes, superheroes get needy
revolutionaries are not above compromise
and jazz musicians must rehearse
before they can improvise

i am starting over
now is my next lifetime
and i am searching for signs

this is how they break you

slit the throat of your native tongue
      legislate your right to breathe

say you have no art
      steal your pottery

call it primitive
      charge museum fee

how many lose home
      land without leaving country?

sanction slaughter
      call it natural order

there have always been
      victims and villains

cage your children
      call them alien

train you like house pet
      pavlov politic

call you less than
      until you concede

if there is no name
        for what they do

how can you be certain
        it is happening to you?

call it reality
        believe it to be true

call it inevitable
        they cannot be moved

call it always have
        something to prove

you were never theirs
        to break

nina and frida enter the chat

these biddies with their deadbolt backs/ take naps
while i construct/ canvas from corset cast

art does not wait until you are well

what they did not understand—the training was classical

chopin, motherfuckers/ carry on like she some backwater bluesy
least common denominator/ reduced me

addiction is not a hobby

no one will hear what i see/ unless they inhabit my body
surgeons don't count/ the wrong lover, maybe

muse is reality

want more than you're given/ be difficult as necessary

loving a man/ who belongs to the world/ is like lying in lava
no one asks if he can/ have it all

let him knock you down/ throw you up
against the wall/ put a frame on it

i don't want the preacher/ i want the pulpit

queen's english

i was born in mount vernon. *money earnin'*
they called it, in the nineties
thanks to heavy d, the most famous rapper from my city

four point three square miles
split by train tracks into north and south
i grew up in a brick house

wished my parents were jamaican
'cause americans knew where that was
from the cornrowed woman
in those *come to jamaica* ads

no one had ever heard of guyana
is that in africa? they asked

i didn't know my mom had an accent
until a friend wanted to know where she was from

my dad's accent is thick,
like the interior, where he worked
in the bauxite mines to pay
passage to a minnesota college
no one gave me a dime, he says

i came to this country with one suitcase
i was not afraid to work

my mother was a school teacher
in a british colony
so slang i brought home from school
was dropped at the door like dirty shoes
ain't is not a word, she would say

the queen's english is real
they will judge you and your pedigree
by the way you speak
it wasn't bourgie,
it was survival technique

when my parents were in high school,
my grandmother, on mom's side,
asked about dad all the time

no surprise, he was a charming chap
says all the girls liked him

mom has a different version
grandma lucy used to ask
'cause dad was always playing cricket
when he should have been in class

two mortgages,
        three grown kids,
                fifty years wedded,
                mostly bliss,
they reminisce

to hear my mother tell it:
he was solid, a man of his word
they came from a common world

to hear my father tell it:
she was a good, god-fearing girl

the following does not depict
any actual person or event

when the detectives come to question you
keep gardening, lifting boxes, cleaning the gills off the fish

new yorkers can't stop moving
you need to pick up your kids

you wish you could be of more help
but you're late for the airport, class

if there's cash on the body, it's not a robbery
every suspect has means, motive, and opportunity

the evidence speaks

the president of the abstinence club could be the rapist
they recycle storylines

it's not the first time the killer is an adult,
pretending to be a high school student

trust your gut

a patriot can be turned
we can't all be good

it's the third law of physics
equal and opposite
can't have the high without the low

if it feels personal,
you're too close to the case

baby, it's cold outside

we are an inevitability
because i called it
like i call the front seat
on road trips
i got shotgun

you the scenery and destination
solved the riddle in my smile
on the first try

didn't have to guess
had the answers to the test
or a copy of the teacher's edition
handed down by an older sibling
who took the same class last year

lashes like daddy long legs
sweep doubt from my cheek
eyes squint to see you more clearly

your lips to my ear
speak words women everywhere
been wanting to hear

we're an inevitability

like growing older
losing baby teeth

you will love me with the same ease
you recite lyrics from your favorite song

the potential of this
is the feeling fifth graders get
when snow falls and starts to stick

you are the prospect of a half-day of school
i am free time in the afternoon

the collective will of a math class
can make the snow fall faster

i called this
the snow will stick

we have the afternoon to ourselves
what do you want to do with it?

the one with the special guest star

dump your baby deer girlfriend and i'll give up smoking and
all extracurriculars except you. what are we waiting for?
middle age? tell your grandma we're having biracial babies. it
won't kill her. if it does, she's lived a good life. my folks won't
care as long as our kids believe in god. they have a specific
one in mind, but there are ways to subvert. childbirth logistics
confound me, but my uterus considers it when you quote
rob thomas lyrics, leave voicemail messages in song. grow a
beard, again. i'll lock my hair, again. let's rent a car and drive
to williamsburg, where we never go, 'cause it's such a hassle
to get there by train. tell me about the teacher who smelled
like rhode island, i'll explain why i stopped wearing skirts for
years. with you, i never have to call shotgun. with you, magic
in the mundane. you know all the scalpers by name. call an ice
cream pillow fight in the field behind meg's house, overlooking
the hudson, where my second love and i saw our ghosts for
the first time. call truce on your family farm in the middle of
the rhubarb. we'll plant something seasonal. see if it grows.
take an afternoon nap side by side. your hand a blanket for the
butterflies. eyes wrapped in yellow caution tape. until i see you,
like city skyline. from every point of view. jersey highway to jfk
descent.

exceptions

i before *e*
except after *c*

the world is flat
the moon is made of brie

or when sounded like *a*
as in neighbor or weigh

lie to yourself long enough
you will believe anything you say

parallel lines never intersect
        the police are here to serve and protect
when in doubt, go with your first guess
        father knows best
forgive and forget

are you convinced of the lies
that you've told yourself yet?

there is no tooth fairy
no easter bunny
no santa claus

planting a flag on the moon
doesn't make it yours
makes a hole in the moon

everything comes back

baby, come back soon
from whatever trip it is you are on

while you are gone
write often, send postcards
i will wait

i have been waiting

waiting up nights
waiting for the jackson 5 to reunite
waiting for black girls to be in style

i may be waiting for a while
but everything comes back

afros, bell-bottoms, platform shoes, you
will be back soon

(i am not so sure
who's lying to whom anymore)

parallel lines curved and in motion can meet
that is a tenet of hyperbolic geometry

e comes before *i* sometimes
in words like *meiosis* and *poltergeist*
where there is no *c* or sound of *a*

this is not for you

in the same way funerals
are not really for the dead
they are for the living to wail and moan
mourn a spirit gone home

in that way, this is not for you

it is for all the rules
we accepted in our youth, unquestioned
myths masquerading as truth

the train comes the minute you stop looking for it

$e=mc^2$
      columbus discovered america
we hurt each other because we care

i before *e*
      everything comes back

except after *c*
      there is no tooth fairy

or when sounded like *a*
      if you have nothing nice to say...

lie

lie to yourself

lie to yourself long enough
you will believe anything you say

but it is going to take a lot more
for you to convince me

you are here.

here is the hole in your bathroom ceiling
roof water rains through

here is the rubik's cube man
you cannot resolve

here is your rented hatchback economy
thunder road on repeat
doing eighty-five on the garden state

here is your last date

here are the shoes, dress, spanx
you will wear for your best friend's wedding
then never again

here is where you think
you could be a vegetarian

here is your first love calling
from texas, hauling fuel
down an eight-lane highway

here is the text you sent
like a twelve-year-old 'cause
you're still too scared to say

here is the phone call you should have made

here is your heart whole
first time since first love

here is the one
you were trying to forget
when you sent the text
to the one who can commit
to everything except you

here's what you learned about truth:
claim you want more
and she will make you kneel
with reverence

here you are

looking for parking
when you no longer have a car

here's what freud has to say:
the hole in the ceiling is a metaphor
for your repressed trauma

here is the space you filled with myth
made real because you believe

here is god giving do-overs

here is your hard pack of cigarettes

say a prayer over your part in things
and lay the past to rest

here is the order of events
here is an alternate theory of the crime

here's the gap
between signifier and signified

here is a sign:
it doesn't end here

jay-z and obama make crust from scratch

i was born by the river
people hold their breath

driving past. same brother,
different body. they worship

the dollar, call it blasphemy
when you start your own church

nothing worth more than
what you're given for free

used to be kids got shot over kicks
no one is going to tell you this—
there's enough for everybody

starting to sound socialist
they're trying to diminish what i've done

everyone has genius level talent,
god-given. we are all his children
i have a daughter now, i understand

earl "the goat" was just as bad as jordan,
but didn't have the same opportunity

can't knight yourself in a democracy
we are a compromised people

what did you expect?

was i supposed to bring world peace?
and what would be left?

thank me

your borough is now a brand

those jerseys aren't a novelty
they represent the team

idle worship

in the middle of your set, sit down.

put your feet up. funk needs a five.
ladies know. heels are sacrifice.

pick up a magazine with your face
on the cover. flip the page. wait

for applause to evaporate like
lace panties, post-show. fellas know.
guitar licks get you laid.

give 'em the grin. the one that winks,
this is what you came for, right?

make them want it. more than vacation time,
health benefits, childhood wish.

stand up, spin, split.
strut to the microphone and blow.

ne me quitte pas
for peter

neither one of us knew french. google hadn't been invented
yet. we asked anyone with rudimentary knowledge what
those lyrics meant. took my parents to see nina for their 30th
anniversary. house lights dimmed. mom leaned in, whispered
to me, *peter cleans up nicely.* nina walked out, wearing all
white. we stood up. i may have cried. if i am being completely
honest, there were tears. that was our song. *ne me quitte pas.*
and *unforgettable.* the version where natalie duets with her
dead father. a new technology at the time.

used to be you couldn't sing with someone who wasn't there.

college, freshman year. mozzarella sticks in the malcolm x
lounge. everyday. we watched *one life to live.* that kid you
went to high school with was playing christian. *that's my part,*
you would say. every day. field trips to the museum of natural
history. anytime the urge hit. when we were kids, we visited
the same museums every year. the arts were important. schools
had a budget for it. bring a brown bag lunch and sit in the
northwest coast hall. sketch a totem pole. create construction
paper replica of ceremonial mask to take back to class. used
to be you could shoot an animal in the wild and stick it in a
life-sized diorama. this behavior is frowned upon now. imagine
an anthropologist swiping your silverware, charging strangers
to come and see. this is how natives cut their grass-fed beef. we
went back with adult eyes. asked why all the people of color
were stuffed.

used to be i liked words because they were not math. so rigid, with its right answers and logical proofs. words could go wherever they wanted, like billionaire playboys and absentee fathers. then i grew up. started to think words were just like math. each syllable with its own place value. i could calculate the correct answer, comma in the appropriate spot.

the only time i have ever seen a ghost was with you. in the field behind meg's house. we were fighting over who would share a bed with jason. who kept things fresh by flirting with us both. we were alone. in the field. sunset. singing. lauryn hill songs we memorized in my parent's mini-van on the ride to rhinebeck. we saw the reflection of ourselves years from now. i was wearing red. you were wearing blue. so were our future selves. that's how we knew. time enough for, *did you see that?* then, they were gone. we didn't tell anyone. if i wasn't there, i never would have believed.

she's saying, *do not leave me.   do not leave me.   do not leave—*

i have been trying to write you, as if you were a memory, something that happened once and never again. as if you were not happening to me daily. used to be i thought everything was a sign. the summer i got my heart broke in barcelona, i had a dream. i was in the desert. a space shuttle crashed to earth. survivors were taken to a local applebee's. then prince showed up and said he was going to play.

[names have been changed]

the call came from diane. who i was not speaking to. because

she danced with sam at the slow jam party. i was twenty-three.
my excuse for everything that happened that year. her eyes were
closed is how i knew. she enjoyed it. more than she should have.
i had laid claim to him like kids do passing cars. *that one's mine*,
i said. and i rooted for joey and pacey. wrote in my journal about
the revelatory season three finale. joey's got a choice to make.
spend the summer in capeside working as a waitress or sail the
eastern seaboard with pacey, in a boat called "true love." no
choice, really. i said, *get on the boat* like it was my mantra. wrote
about joey's courage. not packing an overnight bag, no contact
solution. no concern for what would happen come fall. it was
dawson's show. by every tv law they were supposed to be. joey
was always choosing between dawson and something she wanted
more than him. letting go isn't a one-time thing.

used to be i was a fatalist. in college, the screensaver on my
computer read: *things that aren't meant to happen don't.*
fatalism was a reliable organizing structure. dependable like *law
& order.* follow the formula, solve the crime. your mom used
to say you should marry me. which was never going to happen,
because we both dated men. so we made plans to stand up for
each other at our respective weddings. reenacted scenarios where
the priest says, *speak now or forever hold your peace.* and one
of us would be forced to stand up and make a speech about how
and why the whole sham shouldn't go down. you got married
without telling me. i never got to make my speech. gave you a
best friend break-up mix in a midtown kfc. gave you the silent
treatment for one long, sad week. but you are homer to my
marge and i am gemini to your sagittarius. we are soulmates
and polar opposites. i don't want a life without you in it. so we
make-up, make a pact—nothing breaks us.

we lose touch.

[reason redacted]

then the call.

there is no pretty way to say—

on the phone, you joke about the weight loss, *better than a bally's membership*. and how you're looking forward to rocking a baldy like montel. all summer we make plans to hang. all summer you cancel. i don't remember what i said the last time i saw you alive. one day before your 30th birthday, you died.

no amount of faith or fatalism makes it right. i am never going to stand up for you at your wedding. and who is going to stand up at mine?

there are those moments in life that are a little too on the nose. like if you saw it in a movie, you would think it was trite. *that would never happen in real life*, you would say.

six months to the day you passed, it's my 30th birthday. prince plays a free concert in bryant park. my birthday, my city, for free. *what are the odds?*

i had no idea how i was going to make it through the day. and then prince shows up, says he's going to play. this is not a metaphor. this is god. fuck odds.

gambling

quit your job
>   with no savings
>   and a rough sketch
>   of the rest of your life

withdraw money
>   from your 401k
>   pay the penalty
>   why wait?

in this economy,
>   everything you own
>   is worth more
>   (than it will ever be)

cut your hair
call yourself new
>   call your ex
>   call robyn
>   tell her you bought a ticket to the bay

paso robles road trip wine taste
>   buy a malbec and a tight red tee
>   eat a cookie from an l.a. dispensary
>   chain smoke around bed and breakfast
>   hillside fire pit with san diego newlyweds
>   and vineyard view

go to the water
        with your girls
        and grease-stained bags of burgers
        sit on driftwood sunset

remember you folded
remember your place

spend the night in reno
        resent the safety of the slots
        sit at the blackjack table
        hand the dealer rent, retirement,
        pray god cares enough to pony up an ace

leaving lunch
        on lake tahoe, they say, is cold,
        deep enough to preserve a body whole
        railroad workers, mafia, military
        and possibly a monster, like loch ness

no one can prove it
        ignore the math
        odds are a distraction

what matters is the chip count
        the cards on the table
        the cards in your hand

you must be willing to lose

this one goes out to

i have a rational mind
it has never worked in the past

there is no evidence to suggest
it is mathematically possible for us

but i am an against-the-odds kind of girl

afraid to call the bluff with play money,
but reckless with real dollars

i am bringing back capri pants
and traditional gender roles

i'll be at lunch with the ladies
you make a plan
you do the work

you figure out how to get my attention
while i'm walking home from school
books in hand, wearing a poodle skirt with crinoline

you pitch rocks at my window
while my parents are asleep
cell phones could never
best the balcony scene

you bring lilies, letter, boombox
love that cannot wait for sunrise
some gesture that must be made tonight

you wonder how to make yourself holy
enough for the unearned blessing

you listen to the late night
call in a long-distance dedication

i'm thinking about a special lady, delilah,
she's the one for me

and delilah will ask, *have you told her how you feel?*

and you'll say, *no. but i want to*

and delilah will tell you
to say it with a song

when they reminisce over you
for cindy

you are 1976, the year of my birth
bronx bound, graffiti-covered 2 train to 241st

breakers, beats, rhymes
two turntables, one mic
power from a street light
you are prototype

insist we see de la during finals week,
the year *stakes is high* stickers
covered dorm room door

when i should be studying ordinary
differential equations, stuffing brain like stomach
full of facts i will never need again

you are always *let's go, live now, cram later*
that night at lyricist lounge, rare chubb rock sighting
young mos def rhyming with medina green

we sport tight adidas tops and baggy jeans
scream when posdunos says so

east third papi chulo
feeling your humid, baby blue, late july vibe
he say, *damn girl, your parents must be terrorists*
'cause you are the bomb

you, me, natalie turn around simultaneously
applaud the brother, who won't get the number
but deserves points for catcall creativity

afternoon, after graduation, over green tea
you told me chinese mythology says we are all tied
to our soulmate with an invisible red thread
everyone on earth searching for the one at the other end

i imagine knotted masses of string
mistaking impostors for real thing
even so you say, there is someone
to which we are each connected

so questionable behavior accepted
the clothes he preferred you wear
the phone numbers of male friends he erased
the friday you said you were leaving
the following tuesday you were engaged
the last email from you i saved

...and i miss you
like summers spent swimming in public pools,
forty five-cent good humor bars,
sucking tamarind seeds on flatbush stoops

miss you more than
my best friend from first grade,
the bookmobile, smaller dress size,
mustard flecks in my first love's eyes,
intentions never realized

miss you from 93 'til infinity

plus one...

art of compromise

sun and moon rose
same place, same time

argued about whose hour
it was to shine

while half the world
waited in dark

the one where you have amnesia

we were supposed to have lunch weeks ago, but he cancelled
the morning of. text read: *might have pink eye. can we
reschedule, next week sometime?* i reply: *ok. feel better!* use
gratuitous exclamation point. want him to think i'm sincere.
this is no longer a drama. there is no conflict here. just thirteen
days of radio silence until he texts: *tomorrow?* we go to
frederico's. our lunch spot he calls it. like we are eighty, eat
here every wednesday. the waitress leads us to the main dining
room, all linen tabletops and leather booths. feels like a time
machine, like that polaroid of my mom in a floral mini and
full-on 'fro. i select a booth. he rejects it. i tell the waitress, *i'll
let him pick the table*, loud enough for a woman to look up
from her minestrone. *i didn't want to sit near the bathroom*,
he says. soft like an apology. we order the carbonara and
unsweetened iced tea. what we always get. quiet long enough
to be uncomfortable. *i bought a card because we were
supposed to have lunch on your birthday. when you cancelled i
thought maybe i should give it to my cousin.* he says, *don't do
that.* and then, *pretend i'm your cousin.* he rips the envelope
like a kid unwrapping a new bike. inside—cartoon animals
in birthday hats bounce around. a pink and white iced cake
shouts: *it's your day to celebrate! it's your day to have some
cake!* he leans in. says, *give me a kiss.* vegas becomes vienna. i
hesitate. lean too.

land of make believe

pretend this love is available
behind the bulletproof glass
at any bodega in brooklyn

pretend there's such thing as safe distance
and dawn did not catch you on the subway
sunday morning wearing saturday night

pretend he did not split you like gutted salmon
stomach filleted by switchblade butterfly

pretend it feels fine

in all honesty

if i were to say
i loved you more than cheesecake
that would be a lie

the distance between you and me

your canon is not my canon
your war is not my war
your voice is not my voice

my laziness is your discipline
your restraint is my addiction
your laugh is my downfall

my god is not your god
my memory is not your memory
your scar is not my scar

your past is my guard rail
my want is your question
your map is my misdirection

your up-all-night is my bed by ten
your fire drill is my sleep in
your nineteenth century poet is not my boyfriend

on the midday m-103

i'm an old lady, so you'll have to sit still.
it's nice seeing you now, even though
i thought i already saw you. what is happening with joe?
you know how they blow up buildings? his dad did that
for a living. the child is not even a child anymore.
he uses deodorant, takes his vitamins, everything.
he's going to college, joe. i don't know
the details. it's set in victorian times.
that's when they invented masturbation
massagers. is this 59th street? you were going to leave me
and then i was going to leave you. did you see
that little boy's eyes?

i'm only on instagram to follow drake

drizzy's in a suit, at the club, on a yacht
drinking henny, taking selfies,
making beats, dating thots

i'm in a one bedroom, with no tv
trying to understand the new technology

i have become my mother
who doesn't reply to the texts i send

when did virtual likes become the measure of actual life?
what i need to say is too much to type

drizzy's squashing beef
even his enemies eat

drizzy's on the ball court
shirtless shooting threes

drizzy's making me believe
if i want it bad enough

that could be me
social media celebrity

midwestern teens tuning in
to see my skincare routine

remember the mixtape

is not a question
it as an ode to lost art

drizzy's interrogating
the intersectionality of feminism,
the class divide,
the privatization of public enterprise

i'm in a cubicle
working nine to five

the one where you blow this popsicle stand

if you can hear my voice, clap once.
if you can hear my voice, clap twice.
alright, class. please put your books away.
quickly and quietly. i'm looking to see
who's following directions.
that means no talking, maurice.
you cannot go to the bathroom.
i need everyone in their seats.

i'm going to give each table a deck.
select one person to deal.
if you can't decide, i'll decide for you.
grown-ups gamble with money
sometimes other things too.

how good is your hand?
do you think you can win?
if you don't, you fold
throw your cards in.
sometimes, you know you can't
but act like you can.

that's called bluffing.
i have a terrible hand and pretend.
make the rest of the players believe
they can't beat me.
this card is called the turn.
why would we call it that, shaniece?

good answer. i know that's happened to me.
you're in a car, the driver turns quickly
everyone inside screams
'cause they didn't expect.
whole game depends
on which card comes next.

for the record

side a.

if you believe in destiny
regret is unnecessary
what is was meant to be

love the past the way
you could not love me

memories are more precious now
they are all you have left

collect them like coins
replay the moment we met

like track #6 of sade's greatest hits
is it a crime?

there are no victims here
i was your accessory

tongue tagged name on your neck
to let the world know i was there

you entered effortlessly as air
rubbed my belly when i had cramps

we slow danced like old folks

always and forever embrace
hands kneading my waist

still swaying long after
the record stopped playing

still swaying

side b.
this is where the real hits are
these songs won't get airplay
don't make the pop charts

this is art

open to interpretation
like images in clouds
constantly changing

too wicked to be love
what we made were fast getaways
before the break of day
we made shades of gray
on bone-colored walls

you turn lights on and off
look in the fridge as if you live here
like it is home away from
all other obligations

my friends cannot comprehend
the intricacies of we
why i justify lies

at night in crown heights
truth is irrelevant as s.a.t. scores
subjective as room temperature

love is not all daffodils and open fields
it is a subway seat you politely refuse to sit on
because your ass is bigger than that
you won't fit

you will only piss off the woman reading the *post*
squeezing into a space too small for you

still wake with your taste on my mind
still mistake you for my soulmate sometimes

you are not who you pretend to be
neither am i
that's how we survive

baptism

waded through water
washed salt and sin
still you stuck
grain of sand to skin

yours as much as mine

for walt whitman

thank you
      for paved veins
            transit system of a living body
the city is man
      made now concrete
            asphalt fueled by caffeine,
commerce, nicotine, child
      like dreams of making it
            big like times
square lights over broadway,
      steel scraping sky high
            clouds cumulus say, go
higher, to the man in the crane,
      woman with child standing,
            third car uptown two train,
teen locked in bed-stuy
      bedroom making beats,
            will only take headphones off for shower, sleep

what lies beyond free
      verse? what frontier is left?
            follow the immigrants and indigenous

people from here
      have come from somewhere
            there have always been legal ways to take land

history need not repeat
        the story generations swallowed
                a groundhog day of existence
thrown up into the mouths of children

        black-eyed abandoned buildings
                cars honk, fly like wildlife
sidewalk bubble gum polka dots
        stockbrokers, stick-up kids, baristas, bartenders,
                actors moonlighting as cater waiters, private investigators,
substitute teachers, corporate lawyers, janitors, congenital
        analgesiacs, background singers, post-docs, graphic designers,
                urban planners, bus drivers, nurses, morticians,
the drummer, the front man, the unemployed, the unseen
        price tags on individual life
                some are worth
while others collateral

        it is possible
                we have never been more separate
                        possible we have never been more connected

cubicle cog colleagues conference
        room lunch break
                talk about the job
one hour they don't have to
        6 am alarm clock commute from heights,
                crown to washington,
hamptons summer house, homeless, high-rise,
        blood pressure, bloodletting, upstanding citizens, carry
                laptops, read the *news*, read the *times*, read the *post*,
daydream about never having to take this trip again

satisfied first sip
   coffee rolling about tongue
morning buildings fell
  collective breath held the goodness
    you foresaw settled on our city

nonviolent resistance from the couch does not count
   comrades marry in fifty states
     elected officials abort debate

trash can on every corner
   litter is a way of life
     life is a virtual prospect
the internet is forever, they say
   what about the soul?

occupy everything, inhabit nothing
   this is the artist's task
     nothing into something
immortal

if your life does not fit,
   create another
     pattern from newspaper
like my mother
   on the living room floor
     of the brick house on vernon place

i heard a stranger say she hates poetry
      which is like hearing someone say they hate music
            just haven't heard the right song

they named a mall after you, walt
      might not sound like much
            but it is an honor in this age

i'll be waiting for you
      by the water
            in the shadow of the bridge

the ferry stopped running
      but the subway will take you under
            river roller coaster track

the city will never love you back

rockaway

on the eve of the winter solstice
seven of us stood
in a circle in the sand

held our wishes
and wants
in hand

threw them to the water
where they would float forever
or fall off the earth

in passing

my mother mentions she's going to read a poem she wrote
at the senior center talent show. *you write poems*, i ask.
*oh, you know, i've got a little notebook i write in every now
and then. not as much as i used to.* she insists she's mentioned it
before. i am certain this is the first i'm hearing. both of these
things are true. over the holidays, she hands me a pale, blue
notebook. pages yellow and crumbling. i wait four days before
i get the nerve to open it. her slim cursive slants across the top
of the page, *friday, april 19th 1968, 12:10 am, inspired by the friday
night movie 'young cassidy'.* this is where i burst into tears.
like my obsession with pop culture reference is direct descendant
of my mother's poem about the tv movie of the week. for years
i think there is no relation. now i am certain. her poem begins,
what is the driving force / that causes a man to dream?

the day prince died

cell phone on silent, in my desk.
1:15 pm, 24 new texts.
friends i haven't seen since the nineties
call from overseas. send condolences.
like i lost blood relative.
(didn't we though?)

quote lyrics like gospel. verse
for every occasion—
new year's in spain, rejected
again, bad decision circa 2:45 am,
backseat on the f.d.r., three martinis in.

sometimes, i'd imagine you
as a cashier at duane reade
with head scarf and attitude
ringing up toiletries.

patron saint of all freaks. you are déjà vu. divine
sign i was where i was meant to be. all-star weekend
in vegas. flight delayed, luggage lost. bought new dress
and drawers at macy's in the mall. outside the hotel,
no cabs available. me and my homegirl hop in a limo
with two dudes we don't know. say we're wendy and lisa.
they don't get the joke.

drop us off at the rio. room so small
every seat is front row. mike phillips on saxophone

and your falsetto. serving life
fully realized. genius personified.

we are left with what survives

wake up/ pray/ meditate/ shower hair/ brush teeth/ coffee
sit at desk/ talk to screen/ 'til six thirty
cook dinner/ watch tv/ take out trash/ sleep

repeat

wake/ pray/ meditate/ new day/ same day/ slight change
green tea/ oatmeal/ eyeliner/ lip lined/ feel alive
try not to/ play/ death and devastation mix

what comes up for you in the silence?

new variant/ no plans/ call friends
every night/ an empty folder/ nothing to report/ reminisce
perfect days/ the one with ray lamontagne/ bushwick rooftop/
jones beach birthday/ phone sex/ lunch break/ pray

remember things you don't

how will you/ structure your time today?/ drink smoke scroll
let the destruction be intentional
need routine/ long for a commute/ costume is no substitute for
character

broccoli, chips with ranch dip/ a balanced meal/ watch your
intake
the death and devastation diet/ is killing you/ why self-
flagellate?

the world is sadist enough/ suffering is just change we resist

new playlist/ you were born for such a time as this
if the pen doesn't write/ discard it.

Afterword
The Viscera of Our Times

In Felice Belle's magnificent poem "yours as much as mine," the poet says: "it is possible/we have never been more separate/possible we have never been more connected."

It is as much a question as it is a statement, and in a poem that amounts to a love song to Walt Whitman, it is poignant, provocative, and piercing, as is this whole debut collection.

We are living in the midst of the exponential age, a carousel of quickening, a spin-out of dislocation, and Felice Belle knows that we must, eventually, connect with one another in order not just to survive, but thrive. The times have been disrupted and it is the job of the poet to help us bring them back together again.

Whitman, of course, was the poet of merciful contradiction, and Felice Belle understands this very well.

In fact, there is an ongoing Whitmanesque flair in all these poems, though they are shot through with a distinct orality, making this, for me, a new sort of music. The style is chatty at times, wry, voluble, funny, conversational. The poems thrum with the everyday. They celebrate the new and the now. They are not afraid to dip in and out of pop culture, and then they go off again, soaring in a different direction.

What goes on underneath the poems, and what the reader is left tasting, is a celebration of the multitudinous aspects of life.

These poems, then, get to the heart of the matter, not to mention the lungs and the kidneys and the spleen and the liver too—the true viscera, the blood, and guts of who we are.

It should perhaps come as a surprise that Felice Belle is a graduate of Columbia University's School of Engineering, but it should come as no surprise that she wrote a poem as part of her application.

It is poetry's gain that she chose to engineer a series of different bridges in her life.

I first met Felice through the Brooklyn Public Library where she was a Literacy Advisor in the Central Adult Learning Centre. She worked with adults who were learning to read and write. As the daughter of immigrants, she recognized the lives of other immigrants, many of them low-income and undocumented. Her reach has always been towards justice, especially justice as it is announced through voice.

"My love of theater led me to poetry," she says. "I used to perform poems as dramatic monologues—specifically work by Ntozake Shange, Nikki Giovanni, Sonia Sanchez, and Maya Angelou. Connecting to the work of other writers on a visceral level made me want to create my own. I think there's no substitute for telling your story or the story you most want to tell."

She started reading poetry at the Nuyorican Poets Café in 1997, and was inspired by the poets she met there, and what they did with language. She later became the slam conductor of the Friday Night sessions at the famous cafe.

Felice is interested in the concept of narrative identity— how the story we tell about ourselves shapes and creates our futures. For her, the concept extends to cultures and communities, which led her to her current position as Marketing Director of Narrative 4, a global non-profit storytelling venture of which I, too, am proud to be a part. Felice's words—as well as her actions—help shake us out of the ruts of ordinary experience.

She likes to echo the words of Jericho Brown who said about his last book: "It's the best example of my soul on earth."

Hallelujah for that.

It might be a cliché of poetic perception that the extraordinary gets discovered within the ordinary, but it can also be a deep-down truth. There is a mysterious resonance between the page and the beyond. Good poetry allows us a reality further than the one we ordinarily see.

In the world of physics, scientists often talk about the idea of "quantum weirdness," where an observed particle behaves differently to an unobserved one. So too with poetry.

I found myself, over and over again, speaking the poems in *Viscera* aloud because as much as they work on the page, they also operate wonderfully in the throat. They take me into a frontier beyond free verse with surprising rhythms, interesting tonal shifts, and unexpected echoes. I found, when speaking them, a fury of clarity.

In her Master's thesis, Felice quotes clarinet player Tom Schmidt: "Unless it's a poem not meant to be read aloud—a concrete poem which is a visual experience, say—what's on the page is exactly analogous to what's on the printed sheet of music: a notation or map that is not more than a guide to the music. The musician goes through the notation to get to the music."

Schmidt goes on to quote John Cage who says that a composition is not finished until it is performed.

Cage, of course, is credited with helping to pioneer the idea of the prepared piano, where unusual items—among them tuning forks, screws, spoons, rubber tubes, cardboard, plastic sheathing, bolts, or paper clips—can be inserted on or between the strings to alter the nature of the piano's sound. The music, then, is changed.

And so it is that Felice Belle prepares the piano in this, the visceral world. I urge every reader to risk themselves and speak-sing-sound these poems aloud. Walk around the city. Meander through the trees. Head out to the suburbs of Mount Vernon. Go even to the Walt Whitman Mall and beyond. Bring her poems with you. They will help us all get to very heart of the matter.

Colum McCann

From the Bottom of My Heart

It takes a village, y'all. This book is, because you are. If you're reading this, thank *you*. And my deepest gratitude to—

The Family: Sheila, Compton, Compton Jr., and Carl—for a lifetime of unconditional love and support.

The Etruscans: Phil Brady, Pamela Turchin, Bill Schneider, Robert Mooney, Logan Rock, Aaron Petrovich, Janine Dubik, Amanda Rabaduex—for believing in the work and midwifing it into the world.

The Crew de la Crème: Nicole Barrett, Christina Shanks, Gabrielle Fulton, Natalie Edwards, Syreeta McFadden, Joanne Cheigh, Jon Speier, Jason Quarles, Jamel Brinkley, Will Fisher, German Santana, Vernon Wilson, Byronn Bain, Courtney E. Martin, Isobel Allen-Floyd, Jennifer Murphy, Nicholas Petracarro, Robb Leigh Davis, Kerri-Ann Grant, Robyn Twomey, Rodney McKenzie, Monica L. Williams, Jon Norman Schneider, Ben Snyder, Yael Stiles, Metta Dael, Brent Shuttleworth, Kimberlee Auerbach, Sapphira Al Rais—for years of friendship, heart-to-hearts, open mics, karaoke nights, dance parties, and asking how the writing's going. Martinis on me!

The Vanguard: Carl Hancock Rux, Tish Benson, Willie Perdomo, Nadine Mozon, Paul Beatty, Suheir Hammad, Steve Colman, Craig "muMs" Grant, Universes, Patricia Smith, Regie Cabico, Lemon Andersen, reg E. gaines, Maggie Estep, Liza Jessie Peterson, Everton Sylvester, Tracie Morris, Edwin Torres, Ngoma Hill, Emanuel Xavier, Caridad De La Luz, Eliot Katz, Mike Ladd, Tony Medina, Hal Sirowitz—for ingenuity, invention, inspiration, and making me wish I wrote that, over and over again.

The Nuyoricans: Miguel Algarin, Lois Elaine Griffith, Keith Roach, Bob Holman, Clare Ultimo, Carmen Pietri, Rev. Pedro Pietri, Rocky LaMontagne, Rome Neal, Jefferey Feller, Pepe Deangelo, Julio Dalmau, Danny Shot, Jane Gabriels, Melanie Goodreaux, Yeauxlanda Kay, Alix Olson, Kahlil Almustafa Gasper, Ellison Glenn, Malcolm Barrett, Steve Donaldson, Dot Antoniades, Karen Jaime, Nathan P., Travis Montez, Mahogany L. Browne, Jive Poetic, Carlos Andrés Gómez, Bassey Ikpi, Anthony Morales, Tongo Eisen-Martin, Akil Dasan—for your fire and all those Friday nights.

The Teachers: Sonia Sanchez, Steve Canon, Imani Douglas, Michael Dinwiddie, Fred Moten, Scott Hightower, Denise Stoklos, Carmelita Tropicana, Han Ong, Tracy K. Smith, Tyehimba Jess, Jessica Hagedorn, John High, Lewis Warsh, Patrick Horrigan, Anselm Berrigan, Barbara Henning—for your genius and generosity.

The Famous Writers: Misa Dayson, Steve Gray, Chris Fox, Thyra Heder, Eden Marryshow, Michael R. Jackson, Theo Gangi, Florian Duijsens, Jennifer Gandin Le, Kate Torgovnik,

Scott Lamb, Ethan Todras-Whitehill, Joie Jager-Hyman, Tiani Kennedy, Jake Matkov, Mike Grove, Sarah Anne Wallen—for the workshops, wise counsel, and words of affirmation.

The Artistic Homes: The Nuyorican Poets Café, A Gathering of the Tribes, St. Mark's Poetry Project, Bowery Poetry Club, Cave Canem, Brooklyn Public Library, St. Francis College—for creation in community.

The Narrative 4 Fam: Alondra Marmolejos, Amira Rachouh, Kelsey Roberts, Lee Keylock, Lisa Consiglio, Colum McCann, Darrell Bourque, Faisal Mohyuddin, Shoshana Perry, and the entire global crew—for the power of our collective story and growing wings in midflight.

The Patron Saints: Ntozake Shange, Nikki Giovanni, Toni Morrison, bell hooks, Toni Cade Bambara, Adrienne Kennedy, Adrian Piper, Stew—for reminding me of the limitlessness of our nature.

And for Peter, my heart—none of this exists without you.

About The Author

Felice Belle consumes and creates stories to make sense of the world and her place in it. As a poet and playwright, she has performed at the Apollo Theater, Joe's Pub at the Public Theater, TEDWomen, and TEDCity2.0. Her writing has been published in several journals and anthologies including *Oral Tradition*, *Bum Rush the Page*, and *UnCommon Bonds: Women Reflect on Race and Friendship*. Playwriting credits include *Other Women*, *Game On!*, and *It Is Reasonable to Expect*. She holds a B.S. in Industrial Engineering from Columbia University, an M.A. in Individualized Study from NYU Gallatin, and an M.F.A. in Creative Writing from Long Island University. She is a lecturer in the low-residency M.F.A. program at St. Francis College in Brooklyn, NY and Chief Storyteller for the global nonprofit Narrative 4.

Books from Etruscan Press

Etruscan Press Is Proud of Support Received From

Wilkes University

Youngstown State University Youngstown STATE UNIVERSITY

Ohio Arts Council OhioArts COUNCIL

The Stephen & Jeryl Oristaglio Foundation

Community of Literary Magazines and Presses [clmp]

National Endowment for the Arts NATIONAL ENDOWMENT FOR THE ARTS

Drs. Barbara Brothers & Gratia Murphy Endowment

The Thendara Foundation

Founded in 2001 with a generous grant from the Oristaglio Foundation, Etruscan Press is a nonprofit cooperative of poets and writers working to produce and promote books that nurture the dialogue among genres, achieve a distinctive voice, and reshape the literary and cultural histories of which we are a part.

etruscan press
www.etruscanpress.org
Etruscan Press books may be ordered from

Consortium Book Sales and Distribution
800.283.3572
www.cbsd.com

Etruscan Press is a 501(c)(3) nonprofit organization.
Contributions to Etruscan Press are tax deductible
as allowed under applicable law.
For more information, a prospectus,
or to order one of our titles,
contact us at books@etruscanpress.org.